You can scan and print pictures for personal use so you can color them multiple times or print on a different type of paper.

This book belongs to :

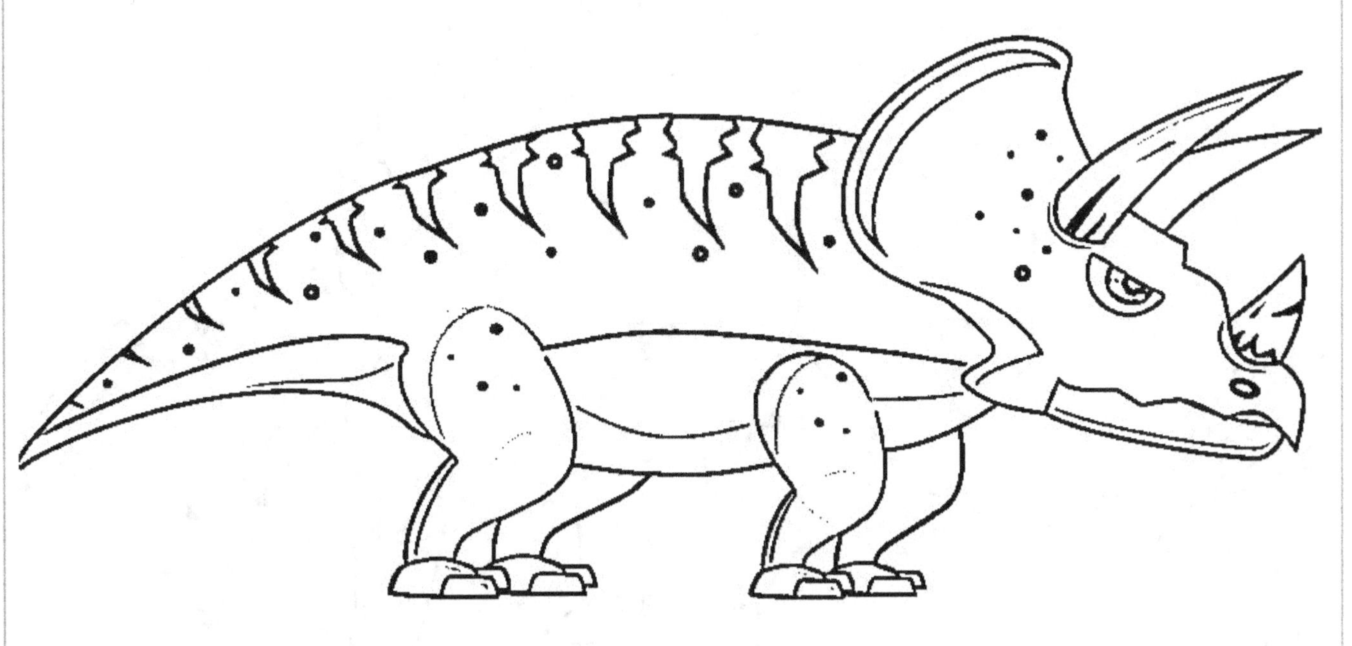

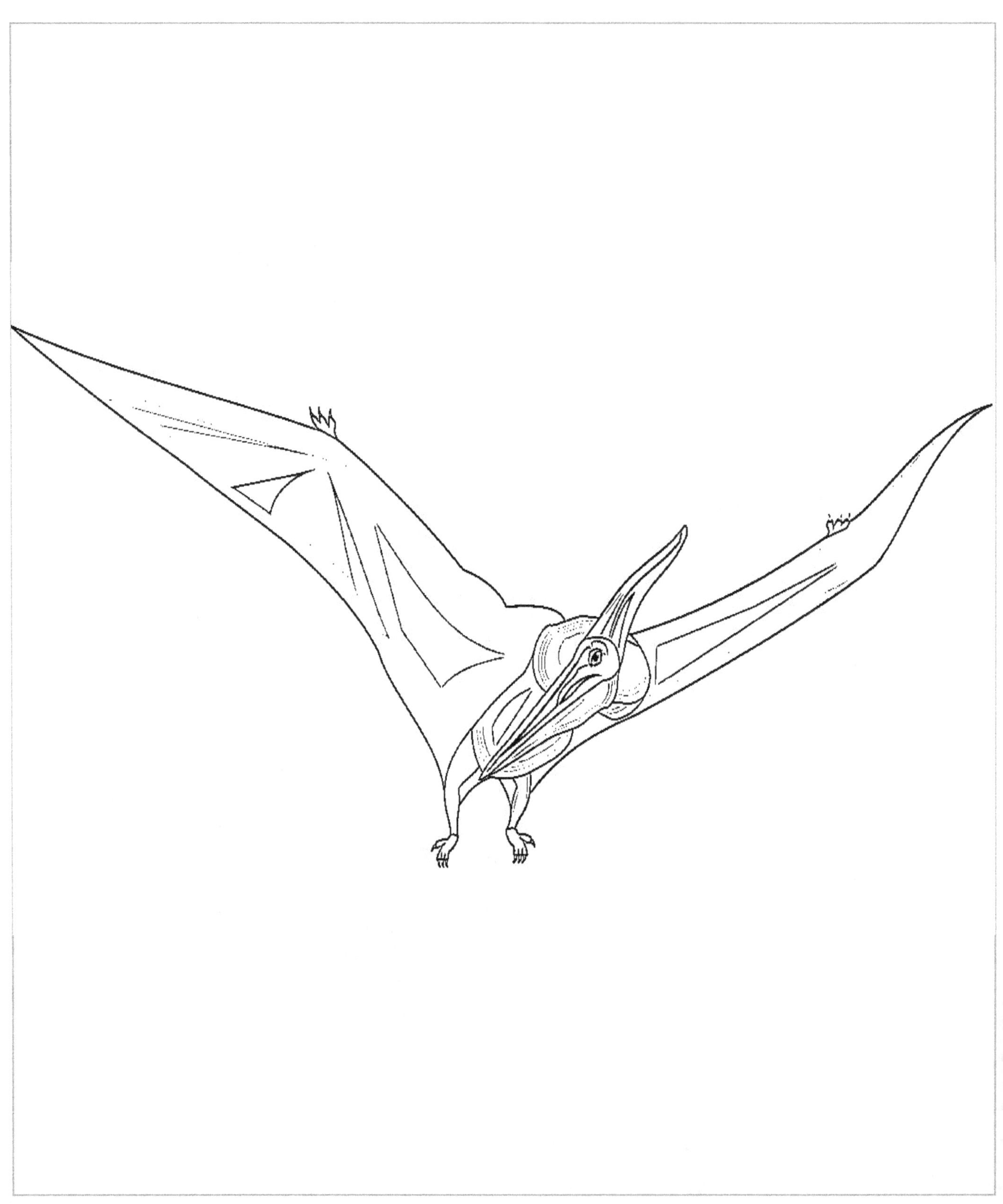

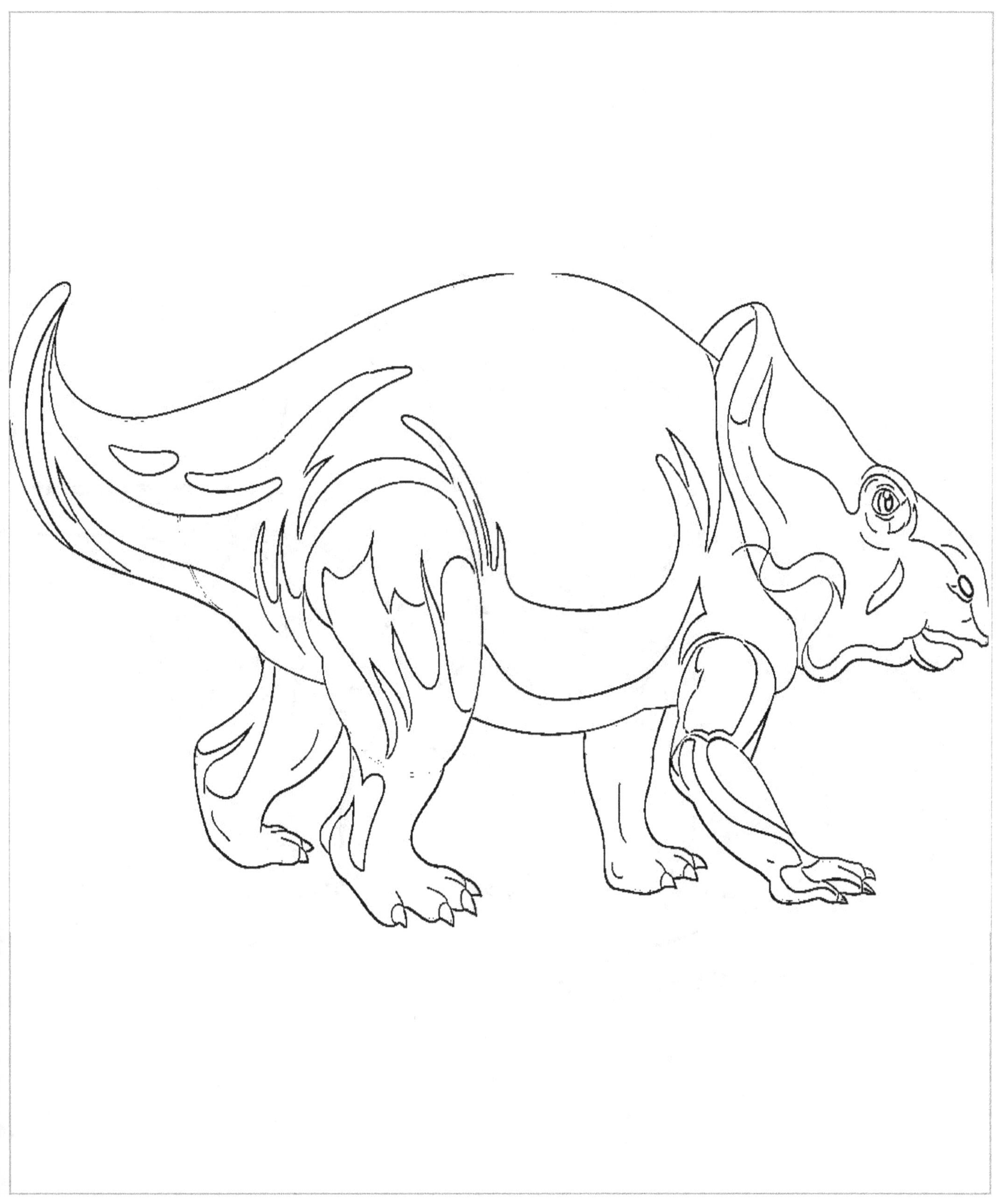

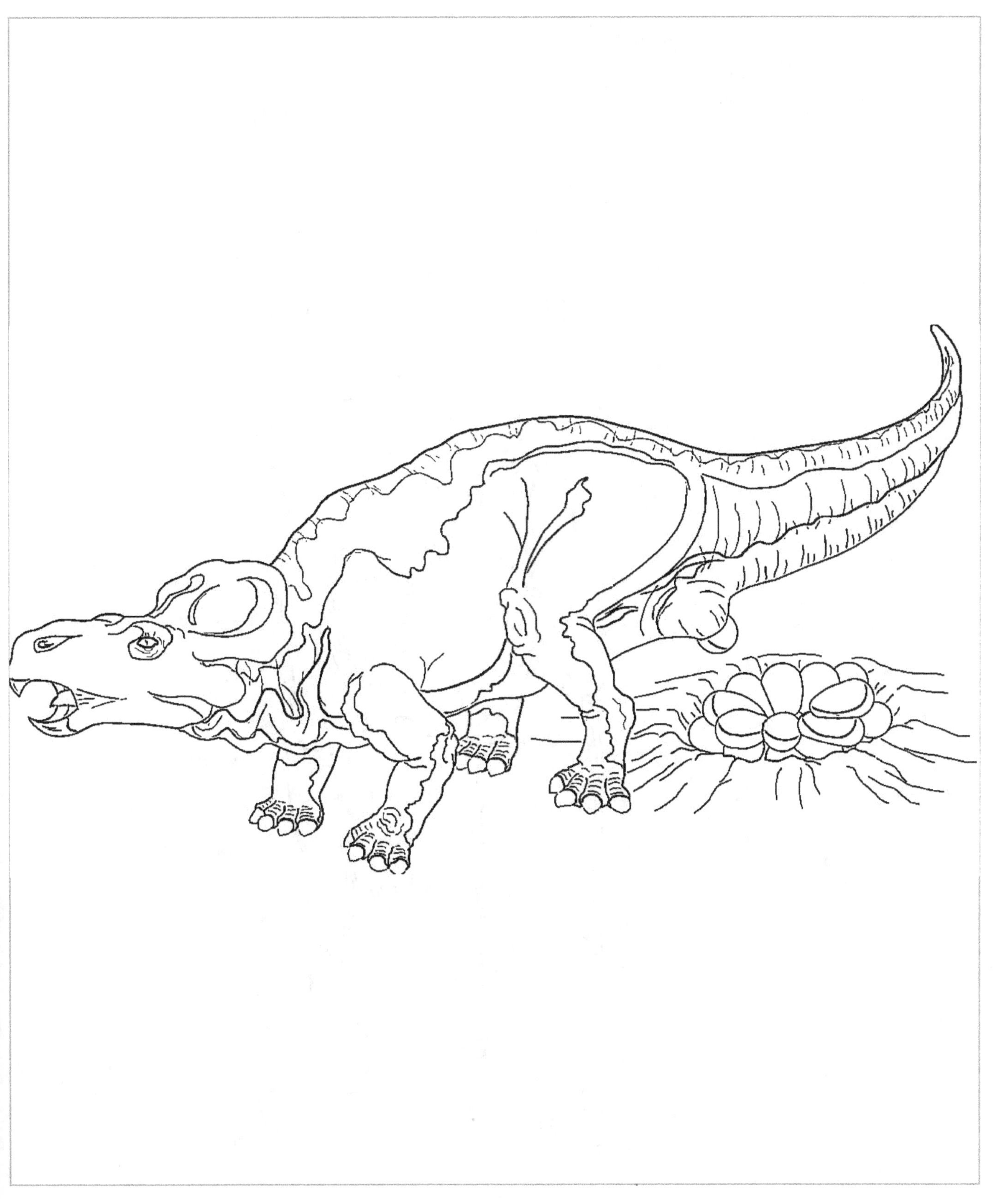

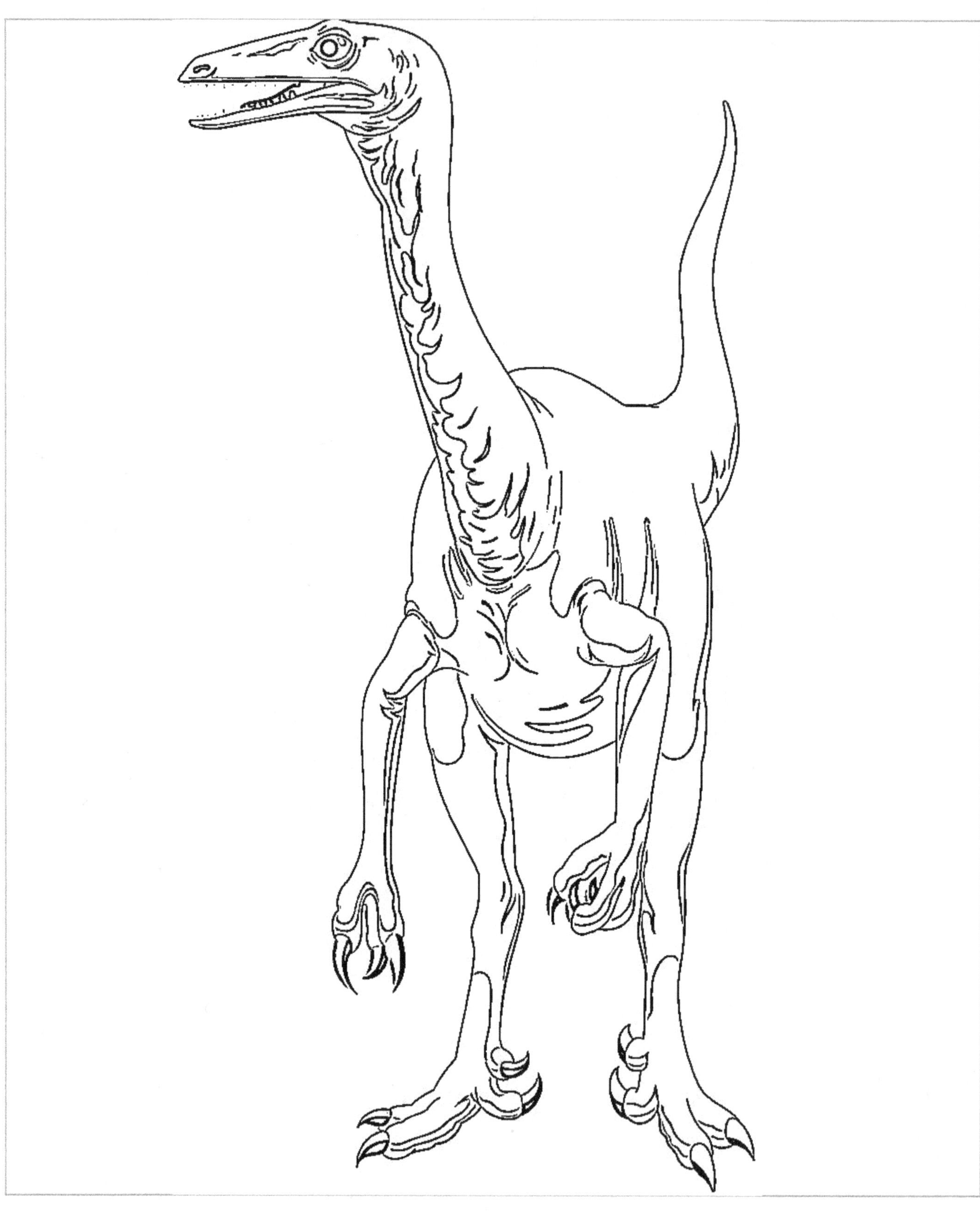

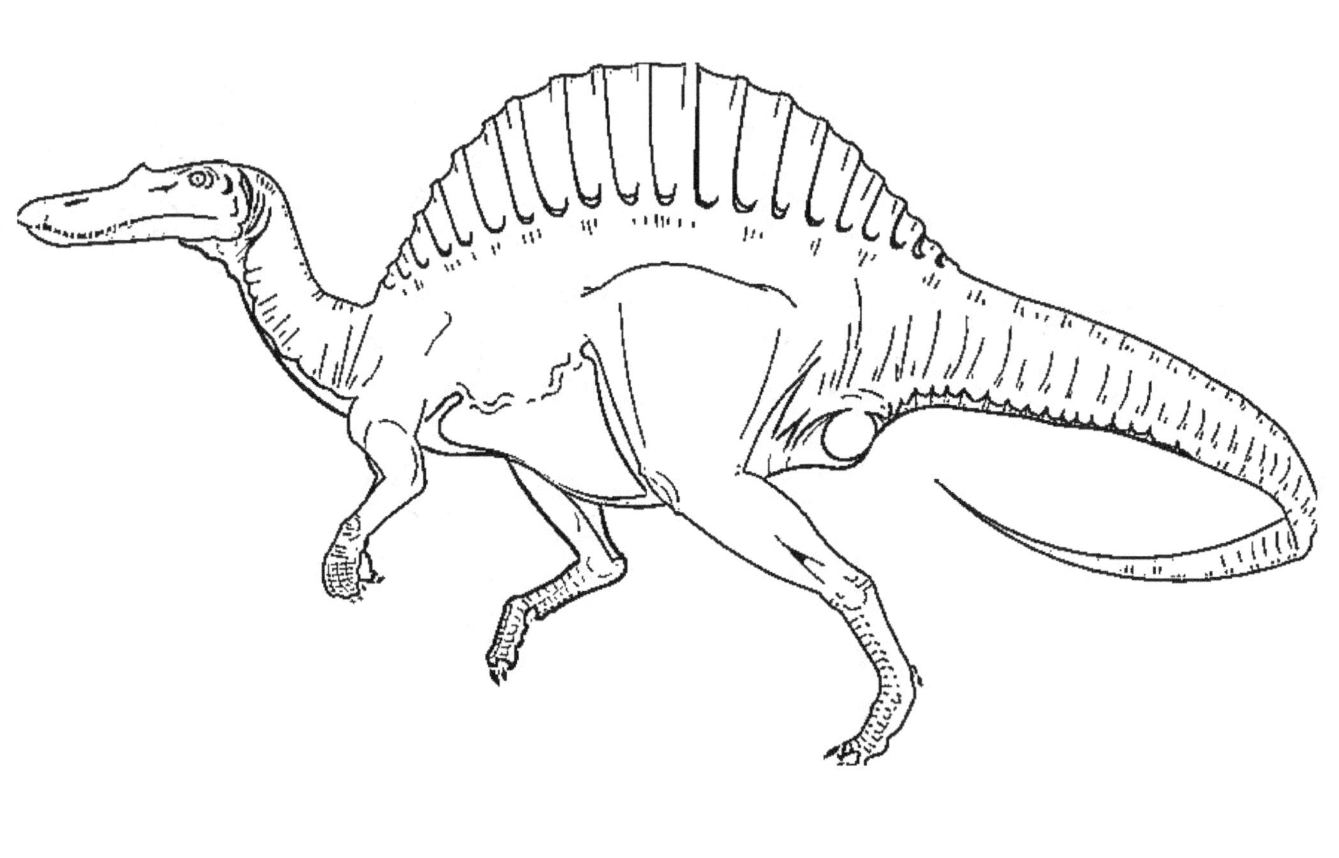

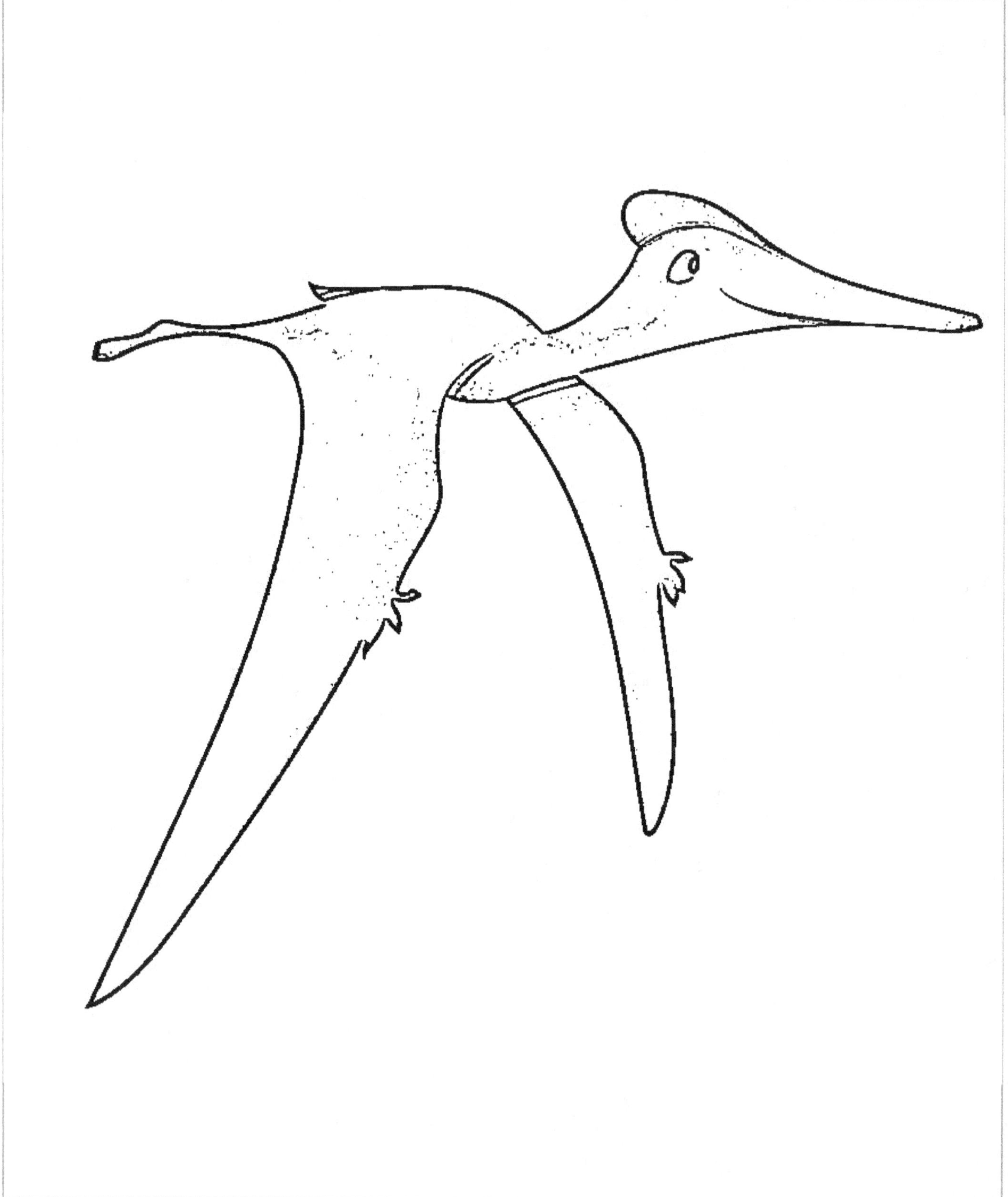

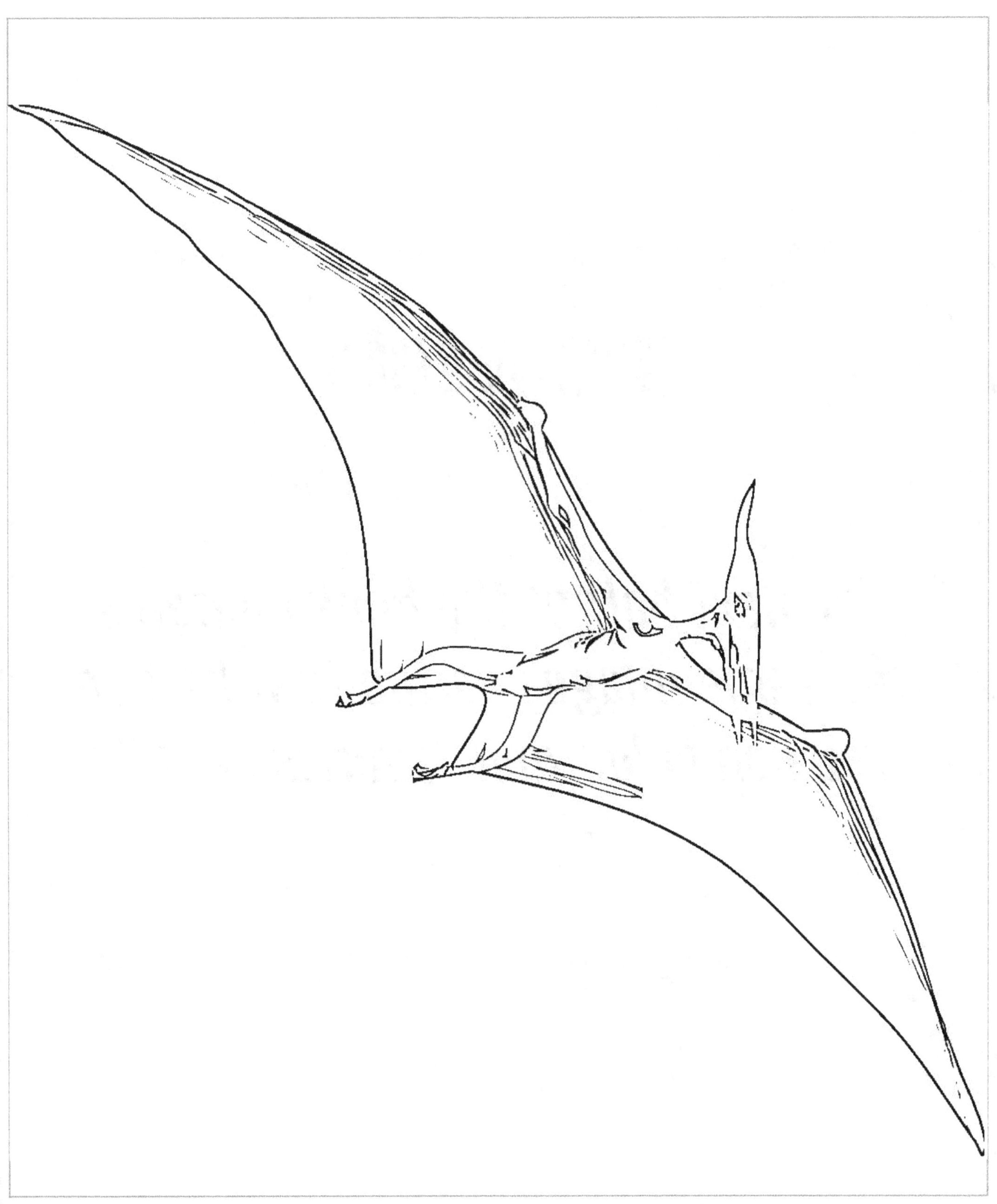

Great Job!

The next half of the book contains the same images as the first half so you can color your favorites again!

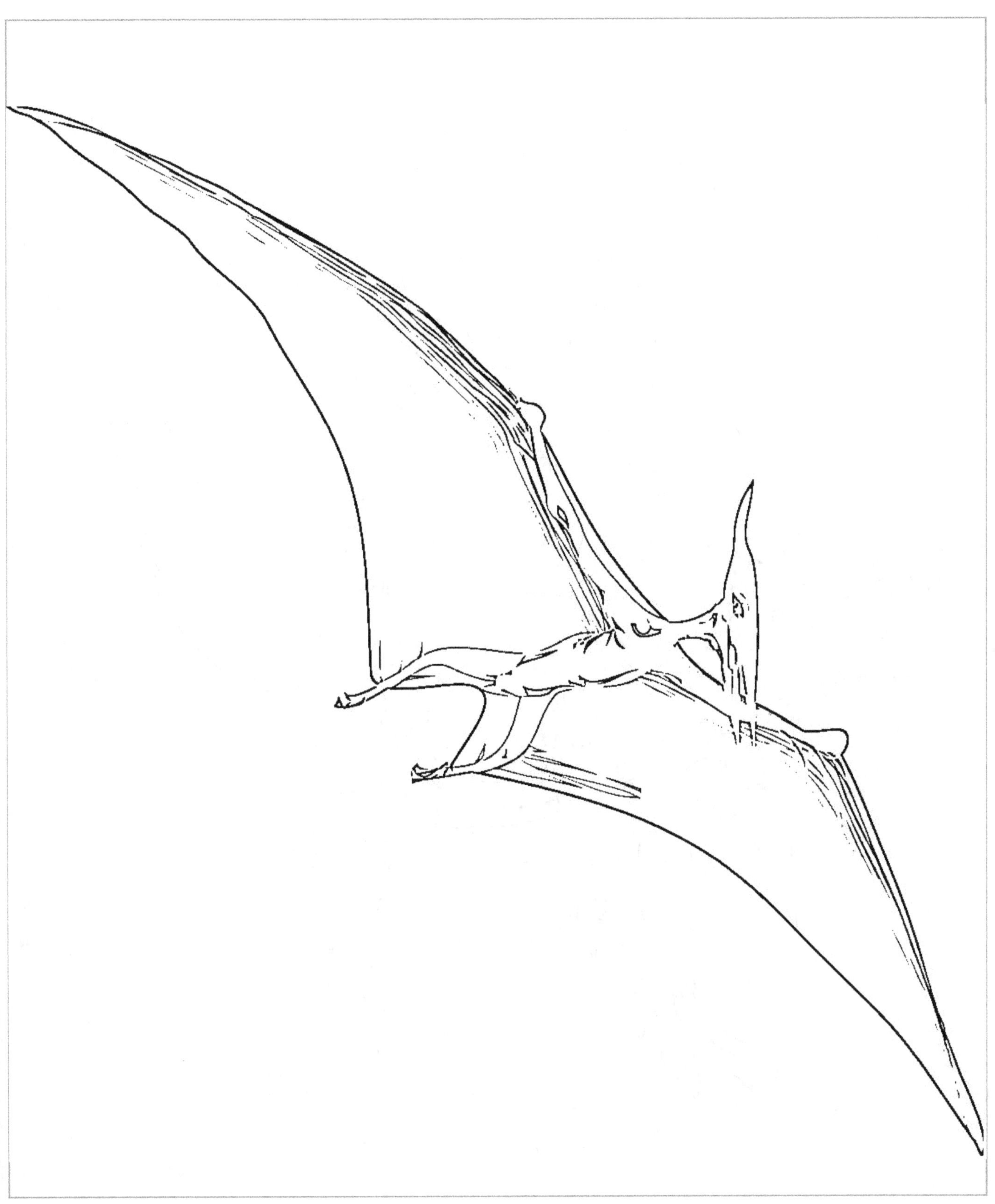

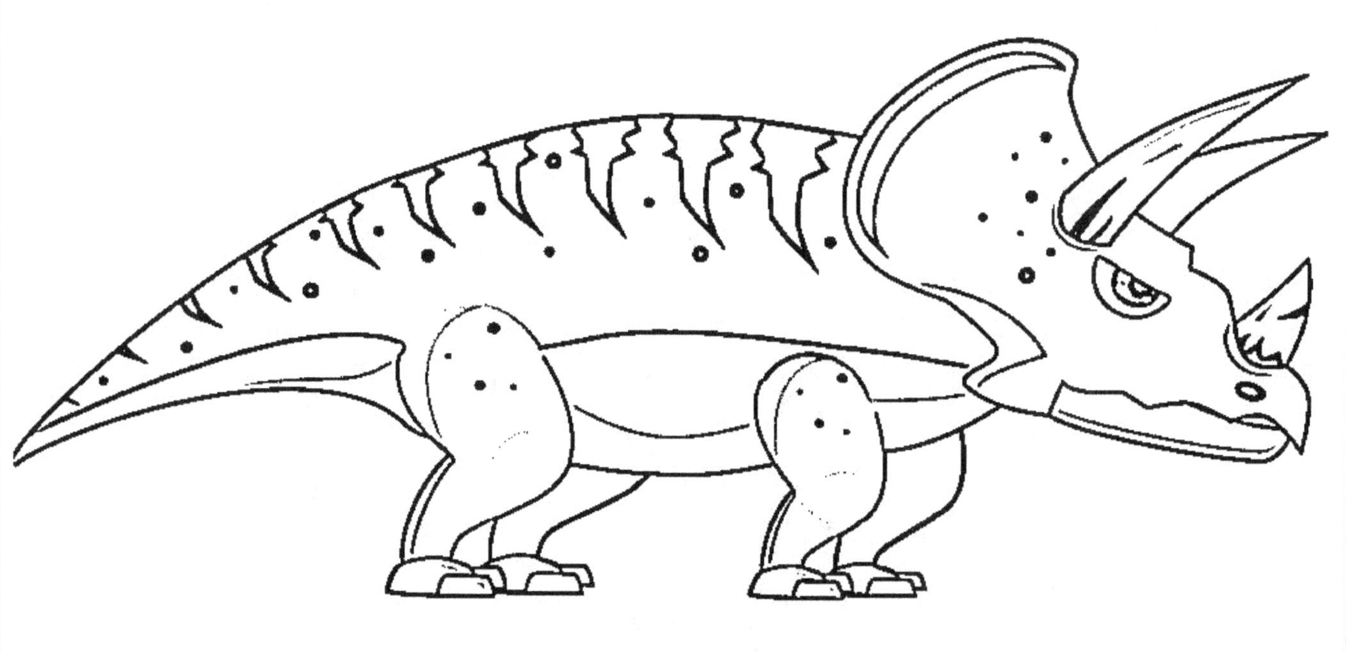

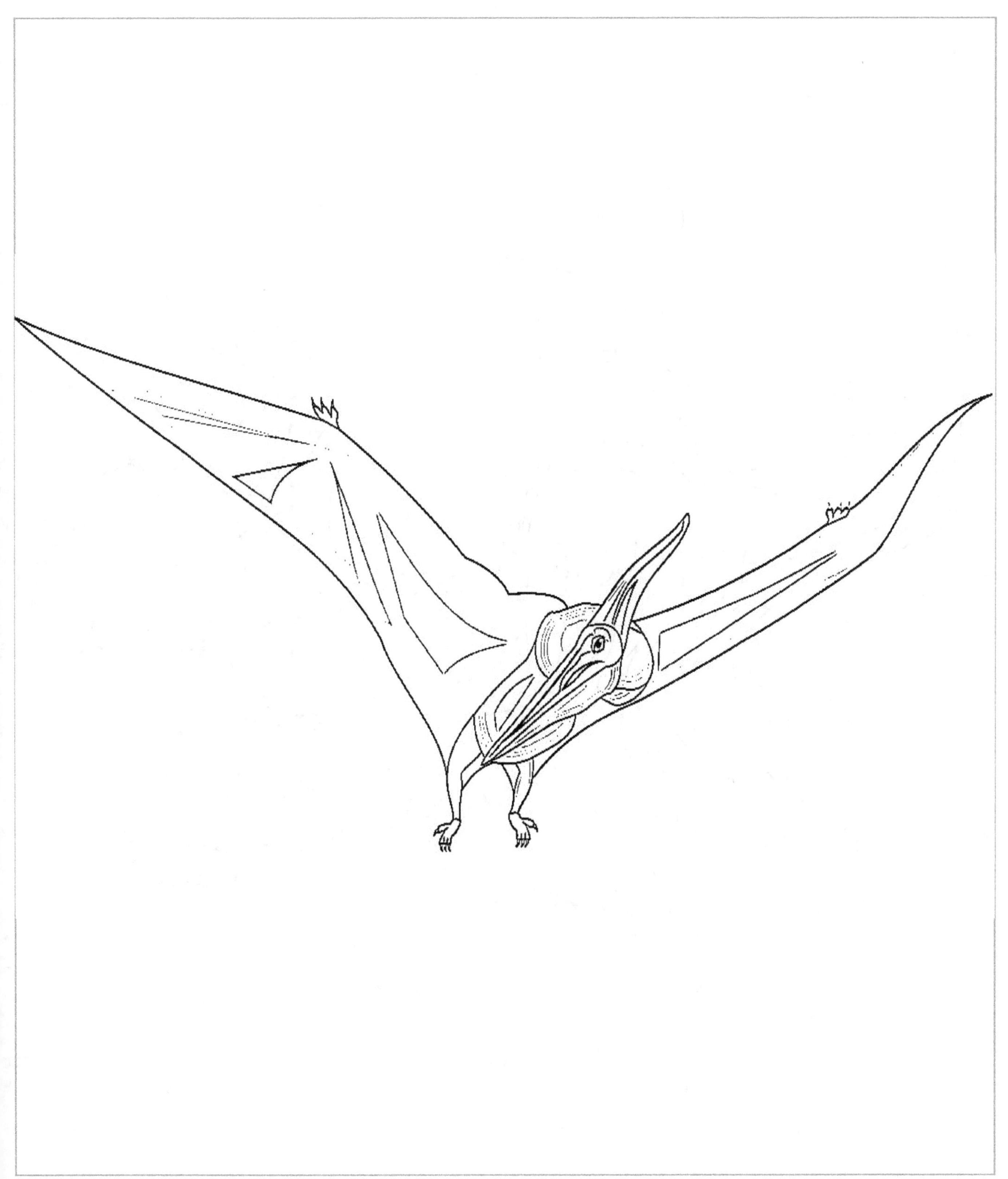

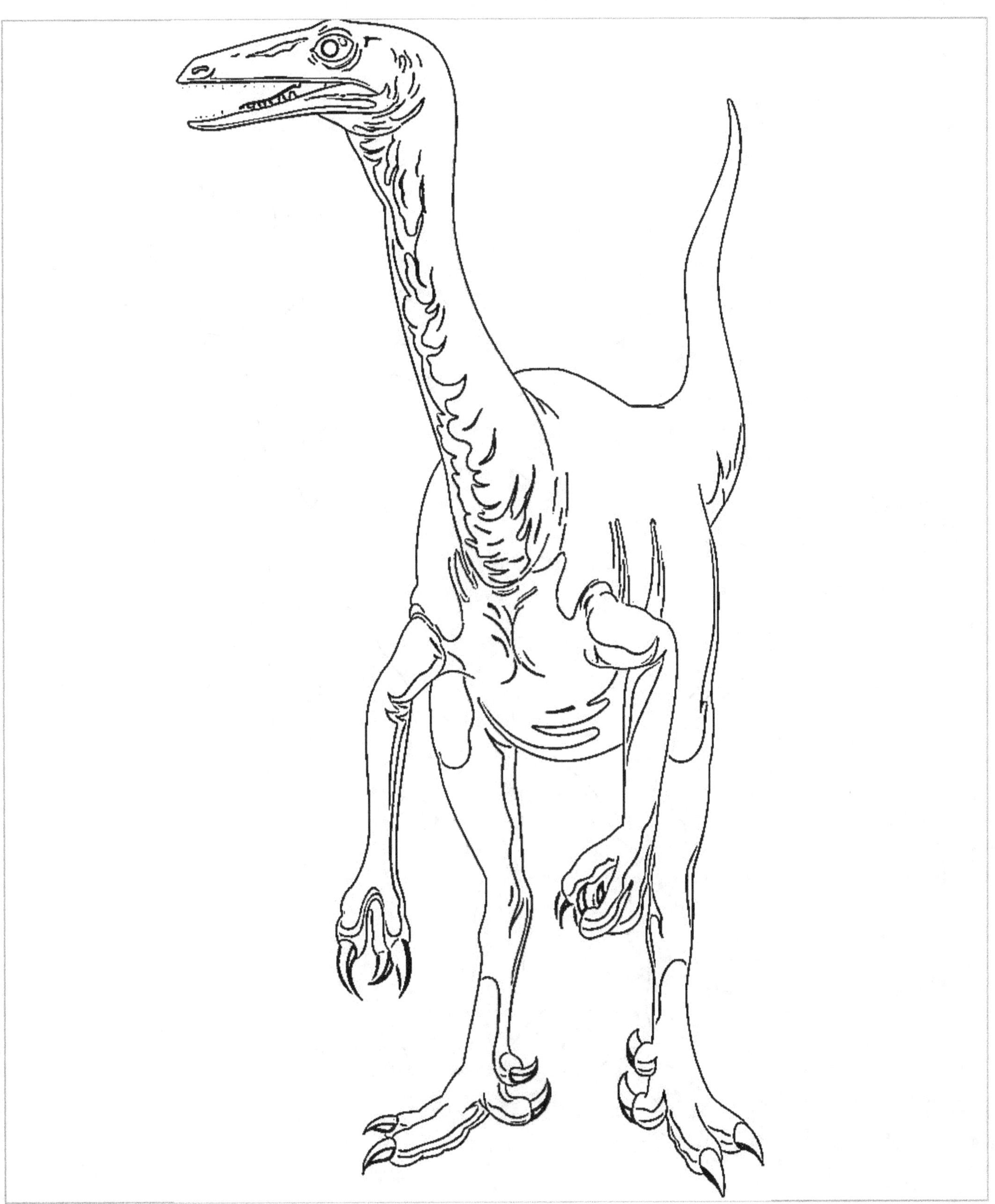

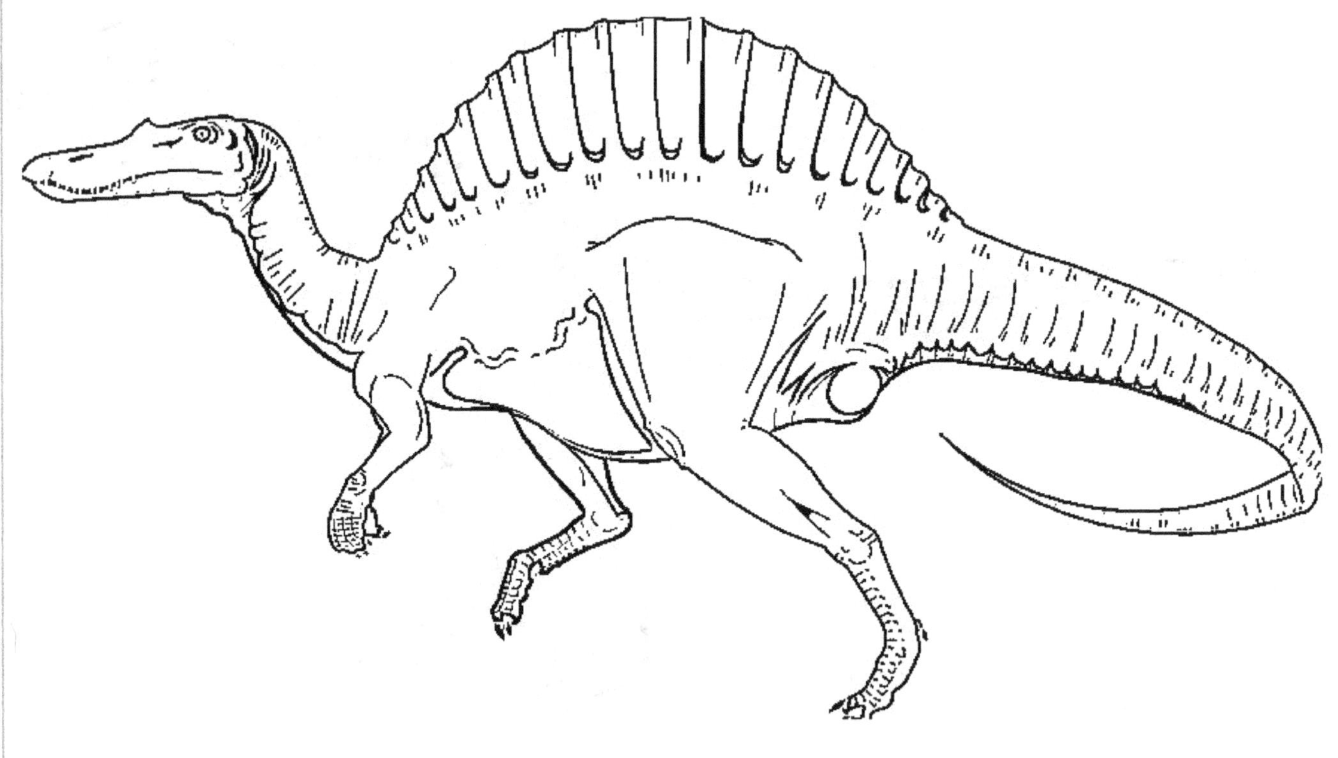

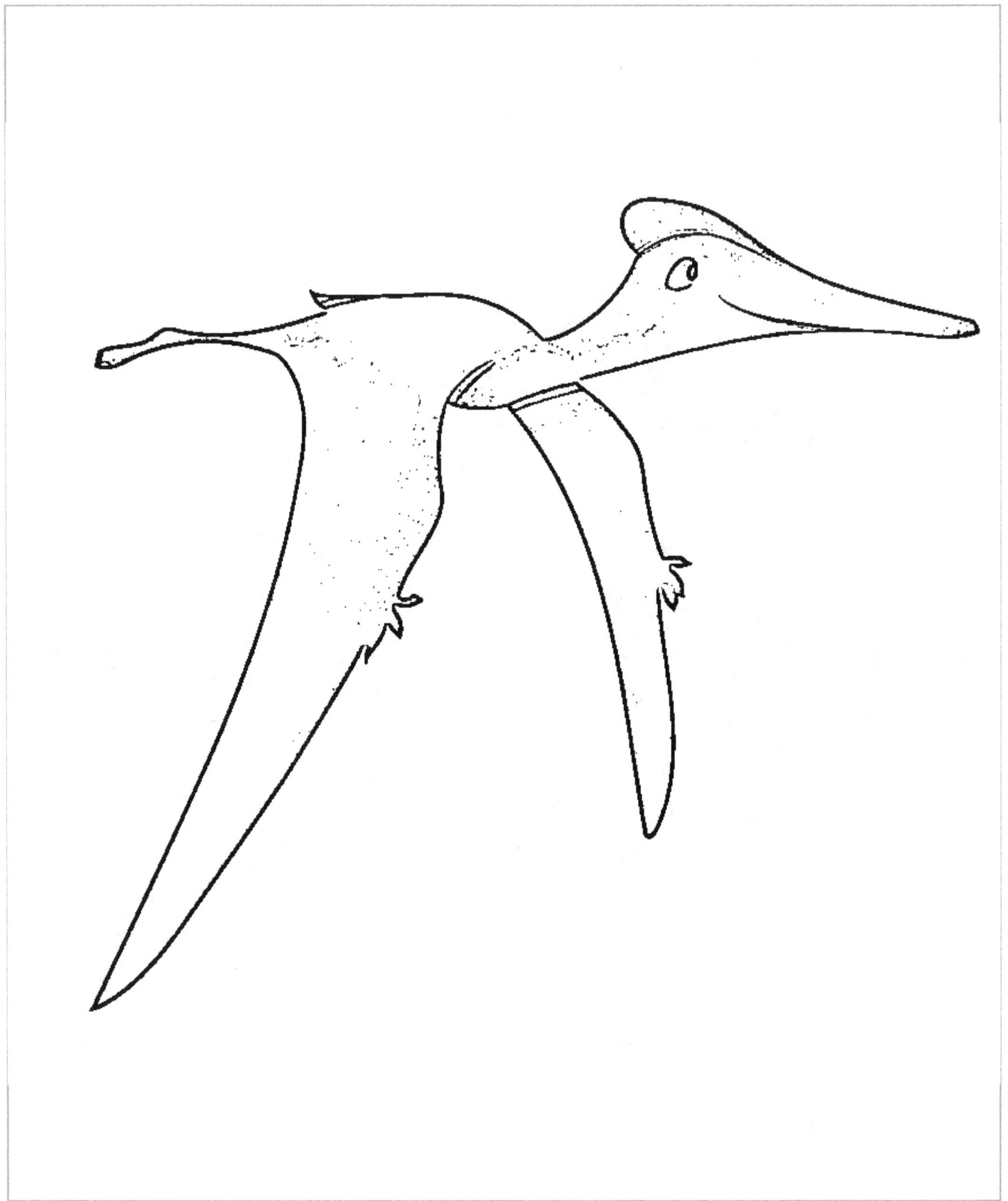

9 798657 715750